DO NOT REMOVE
CARDS FROM POCKET

Great Careers for People Who Like Being Outdoors

by
Helen Mason

U·X·L

An Imprint of Gale Research Inc.

An imprint of
Gale Research Inc.
835 Penobscot Bldg.
Detroit, MI 48226

Library of Congress Catalog Card Number 93-78075
ISBN 0-8103-9390-5

The activities in this book have been
tested and are safe when carried out
as suggested. The publishers can
accept no responsibility for any
damage caused or sustained by use or
misuse of ideas or materials
mentioned in the activities.

Acknowledgments
The author and the publishers wish to
thank those people whose careers are
featured in this book for allowing us
to interview and photograph them at
work. Their love for their chosen
careers has made our task an
enjoyable one. We are very grateful
to the following people who provided
contacts, coordinated interviews, and
assisted with photographs: Dan
Crawford, Ron McHugh, and Lou
Short of Ontario Hydro; Douglas
Magee, Brian Kahler, and Dennis
Stossel of Atmospheric Environment
Service, Government of Canada; Bud
Weiner of Northern Illinois
University; Robert Keir; and Gary
Ball.

Design concept: Julian Cleva
Design and layout: Warren Clark
Editors: Rosemary Tanner, Jane McNulty
Proofreaders: Diane Klim, Anna Marie Salvia

Printed and bound in Canada
10 9 8 7 6 5 4 3 2 1

This book's text stock contains more
than 50% recycled paper.

Contents

Barry Peltier

Practical Forester

PERSONAL PROFILE

Career: Practical forester. "Trees can cause fires or electrocute people if they grow into power lines. I'm responsible for making sure this doesn't happen."

Interests: Hunting, fishing, and carpentry. "I recently built a small office for my aunt, who owns a gas station."

Latest accomplishment: Qualifying as a practical forester after a five-year apprenticeship.

Why I do what I do: "I grew up in the country, where I was always outside — playing, biking, spending time at a bush cabin. I like being outdoors."

I am: Quiet, shy, and hard-working. "I like to work with my hands. If I don't get a lot done during the day, I try harder the next day."

What I wanted to be when I was in school: "An auto mechanic. I really enjoy working with machines."

What a practical forester does

Thousands and thousands of power lines crisscross North America. Many of these power lines run above or beneath city streets. Long lines cross farming and forested areas as well. "Brush and trees can grow into the wires," says Barry Peltier. "As a practical forester, I trim trees and control vegetation under the wires. I work for a power company that owns the lines."

Trimming trees

"You have to know how trees grow in order to trim them properly," Barry explains. "Poplars can grow almost 2 m in a year. Therefore, I cut a lot more off a poplar than I do from an evergreen, which may grow only 30 to 40 cm per year.

"In my job, I also consider the time of year. Power lines are made of metal, so they expand during hot weather and contract when it's cold. As a result, they sag during hot summer days. If I'm cutting branches in winter, I must remember to trim a little more off these branches.

"When I'm trimming a tree, I stand back and form a picture in my head of how I want the tree to look afterwards. Then I figure out what and where to cut in order to get what I want. If I have to cut the top off a tree, I'll prune the side branches so that it looks as though the tree grew that way naturally.

"Sometimes a rotten or damaged tree must be removed. When this happens, we cut and stack the wood so that the property owner can use it. Small branches are made into wood chips that people use as garden mulch. The power company may offer to plant another tree a little farther away from the lines."

Safety is important

"Tree trimming can be dangerous, because many of the branches are close to live electrical wires," Barry cautions. "I had to take a special safety course before I could work close to a live power line."

Electricity always takes the shortest path to the ground. It can pass easily through a human body. That's why people working near electricity wear special boots. These boots have a layer of rubber that acts as a barrier between the electrical current and the ground. This keeps the current from passing through a person's body.

Brush control

"To control the plants growing under power lines, we use mechanical or chemical methods," Barry explains. "Mechanical methods include pruning or cutting down trees and bushes. Trimming by hand takes a long time and costs a lot of money. Also, when we cut a tree, small suckers grow around the stump. We have to cut these again later."

Herbicides are chemicals that kill plants, roots and all. "We use herbicides much more carefully than previously," notes Barry. "We spray only the plant we need to kill, so that we don't harm the surrounding environment.

"As a safety precaution, when using herbicides, we wear coveralls, boots, hard hats, goggles, and rubber gloves. With our goggles on, we look like human-sized ants!" laughs Barry.

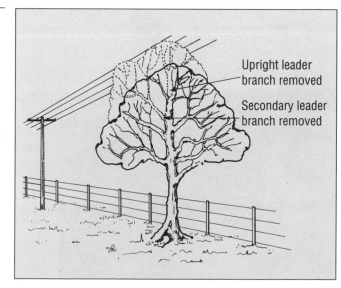

Barry examines a tree's branches to identify the "leader" branch. This branch grows straight up from the top of the trunk. The leader branch is removed at the trunk.

Upright leader branch removed

Secondary leader branch removed

All in a day's work

"Each morning, I meet my crew in the company shop and greet my partner for the week. Because the work is dangerous, we use a buddy system: I always work with a partner. The partners are assigned from the nine or ten people on my crew. Since we change partners on a weekly basis, we have to get along well with everyone.

"First, we get our orders from the job supervisor. Then I collect and check my equipment: Does the chain saw need fuel? Is the oil at the correct level? Is the pruner sharp? I also check that all equipment is clean and dry. If the equipment is dirty or wet, it could conduct electricity. When we're using a bucket truck for high trimming, I clean and wipe down the boom.

"When I drive the company truck, I always do a 'circle check' before we leave: Are the tires in good condition? Do the signals work? Are the belts tight? Are the brake, oil, and transmission fluids at the correct levels? I do minor repairs myself, and make a note of major things that a mechanic should check. My mechanical background helps a lot here."

Remember safety gear

"Last thing before I leave the shop, I pick up my safety equipment for the day. I always wear a hard hat and gloves. When I'm going to use a chain saw, I add earplugs, safety glasses, and chain saw chaps to protect my legs in case the saw blade jumps.

"As soon as we reach the job site," Barry explains, "we have a tailboard conference. The supervisor reviews the hazards of the job we're doing, and tells us what precautions to take. If there's steep terrain, for example, he reminds us to stop the chain saw before walking anywhere.

"After the conference, my partner and I start the day's work. We sometimes work side by side. On other jobs, I do the work while my partner watches for safety hazards — then we switch.

"This is especially important when we're doing aerial work. It takes a lot of concentration to climb a tree and place the ropes so that we can take down large branches without damaging nearby power lines or buildings. My buddy makes sure my safety rope is in the right place. If it isn't, and I slip, it's a long way down!

"This spring, I had an accident that has made me even more cautious. I was concentrating so much on getting the ropes on a tree that I forgot to check my own safety rope. I took a wrong step and fell out of the tree. Luckily, I landed on a pile of branches that broke my fall. Now, the crew teases me about the fastest way to come down a tree."

Barry uses a chain saw close to some live wires. As he works, he stands in a bucket that is raised or lowered on a boom. He's glad to know that his partner, who is operating the boom, is keeping an eye on him.

Varied shifts

When working in town close to the company office, Barry works eight-hour days, with a half-hour for lunch. When working out of town, he works four 10-hour shifts, then has a three-day weekend.

"Occasionally, we have to stay on a remote job site for a week. A company plane drops us off early Monday morning and picks us up in time for the weekend," Barry notes.

"If there's an emergency, such as an ice storm that knocks trees into power lines, we're called in to help. It sure is cold when you're cutting up a tree with the snow falling and the wind howling around you."

Fighting cold weather

When people work outdoors in winter, water vapor from their breath can condense on glasses or facial hair, causing minor discomfort. When you dress for winter weather, layer your clothing so that you can take off items as you begin to perspire. Then put the layers back on when you stop for a break.

Frostbite occurs when parts of the skin are frozen. The skin becomes white or waxy in appearance, and feels numb. If you get frostbite, thaw the area slowly by placing it in lukewarm water.

Activity

Can I work in the cold?

When Barry trims trees in winter, he dresses warmly. But if he needs to adjust his chain saw, he may have to take off his gloves for a while. Try this experiment to find out what it might feel like to work with your hands in cold weather.

You will need

2 or 3 trays of ice cubes
plastic pail half-filled with cold water
shoes with shoelaces
thermometer
watch with a
    second hand
towel

Procedure

1. Time how long it takes you to tie your shoe laces. Then untie the laces.
2. Record the temperature of the cold water. Soak your hands in this water for 2 minutes. Now tie your shoe laces again. Record how long it takes this time.
3. Add half a tray of ice cubes to the water. Measure the temperature of the water. Soak your hands in the water for another 2 minutes. Tie your shoe laces, and record how long it takes. Untie the laces.
4. Repeat this exercise. For each half tray of ice cubes, record the water temperature and the length of time it takes you to tie your laces.

How to become a practical forester

After graduating from high school, Barry took a course in heavy-equipment mechanics. "I couldn't get a job," he recalls, "so I looked into other types of work. I found a job as a skidder operator for a logging company. I ran a large machine that hauls cut trees out of the bush. I loved being outside, but I didn't want to spend the rest of my life in the bush."

Apprenticeship training

"One day, I saw an advertisement for forestry apprentices for a power company. I applied, and worked as an apprentice with experienced workers for five years. I did hands-on work for the company's forestry department. For a couple of weeks every year, I attended training school. The instructors had been in the trade for a long time. It was great learning from people with experience like that."

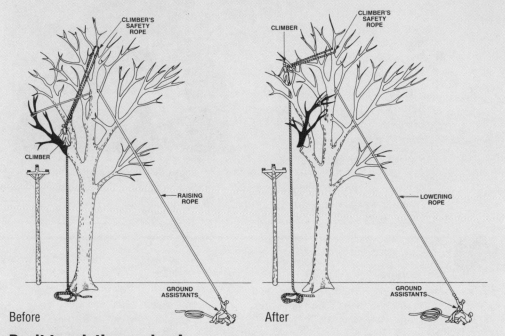

Before — After

Don't touch those wires!

Some branches grow directly over power lines. Barry has to figure out how to remove a branch without touching the wires. He ropes the branch, then runs the rope up and over a higher branch. Two crew members help by raising the branch as it is cut. Notice that Barry's safety rope runs above the path that the falling branch will take. Barry has to make sure that the other ropes do not interfere with his safety rope.

Once the branch has been cut, Barry climbs out of the way while his partners lower the cut limb. What other branches will he have to cut?

Is this career for you?

"I love my work," Barry says. "I enjoy being outdoors. I also enjoy working with machinery. We use chain saws, pruners, spraying equipment, and all-terrain vehicles when doing heavy work in isolated areas.

"This job wouldn't suit everybody. I'm lucky that sub-zero temperatures don't bother me. As long as I work steadily, I can keep warm. But some people have a hard time in cold weather.

"In my job, it's important to be in good physical shape. It takes strength and agility to climb trees. Active sports are a good way to increase your endurance. Team sports are good training, because a lot of this job includes team work. When my partner and I are working around high tension wires, we depend on each other for safety. Experience in team sports teaches you to be aware of what other people around you are doing."

Career planning

Interview a practical forester. Ask about the safe use of chain saws, and about how to remove dead trees and tree branches without doing a lot of damage.

Making Career Connections

Interview someone who works outside in extremely hot or extremely cold weather. What precautions does the person take in these conditions?

Some forestry techniques involve levers. Read about how to use levers. A librarian can help you find information.

Try to obtain a summer job on a forestry crew or with a gardening company. Learn as much as you can from the other workers.

Getting started

Interested in being a practical forester? Here's what you can do now.

1. If you know someone who cuts firewood, volunteer to help when a tree is cut down.
2. Offer to help at a local garage or shop to learn about maintaining small engines.
3. In a library, find a book about knots. Practice tying knots, using both string and heavy rope.
4. Join a mountaineering or rock-climbing club. Learn how to climb safely, using ropes.
5. Learn how to handle emergencies by taking courses in First Aid and cardiopulmonary resuscitation (CPR).
6. In school, take hands-on practical science courses. In physics, you'll learn about electricity. In chemistry, you'll learn some precautions to take when working with chemicals.

Related careers

Here are some related careers you may want to check out.

Forester
Studies trees and their relationships with each other and their environment. Advises individuals, companies, and governments on ways to keep a forest healthy. Often does research on new ways to use lumber; for example, using waste sawdust to run a car engine.

Forest fire technician
Organizes the crews that fight forest fires. Arranges necessary supplies, transportation, and communications. May also talk to the public about how to prevent forest fires.

Maple syrup producer
Maintains a maple forest throughout the year. "Taps" trees in early spring to allow some of the sap to run through tubes to the "sugar shack." Boils sap to make maple syrup and maple sugar. Maintains syrup-making equipment. Markets maple products.

Future watch

There are many secure, long-term positions in practical forestry. As people become more and more concerned about the possible effects of chemical controls, the number of practical foresters will increase. Practical foresters will be needed to trim all the trees and bushes that are currently controlled by chemical methods.

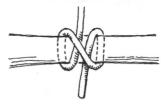

Barry's favorite knot is a clove hitch.

Ellen Heale

Environmental Horticulturist

PERSONAL PROFILE

Career: Environmental horticulturist. "Many human activities damage the environment. I help to undo this damage."

Interests: Gardening, stained glass, reading, travel, home renovation. "Right now I'm stripping and refinishing all the woodwork in my house."

Latest accomplishment: Judging the national finals of a Science Fair.

Why I do what I do: "I get a real feeling of accomplishment from seeing barren land brought back to productivity."

I am: Well-organized, decisive, responsible, a problem solver, and a good communicator. "When things get tough, I'm good at crisis management."

What I wanted to be when I was in school: "I didn't have a clue! I just knew it had to be related to science."

What an environmental horticulturist does

Many human activities, for example, mining, logging, and heavy industry, can damage the environment. Natural factors, including forest fires and droughts, can also cause harm. Environmental horticulturists find ways to improve damaged areas so that plants can grow again.

"I'm responsible for growing plants on huge piles of ground-up rock," says Ellen Heale. "I work for a large nickel-mining company. All that rock comes out of the mine. It has to be crushed before it goes through the 'smelting' process to separate out the nickel."

Once the nickel has been removed, the leftover rock is known as "mine tailings." Thousands of tonnes of this ground-up rock are dumped in large areas called tailing dumps. Plants cannot grow on these sites, and the tailing particles erode easily — blown away by wind and washed away by rain.

Some techniques used to separate nickel from rock release sulfur dioxide into the air. This gas can bleach and burn leaves, such as this zucchini leaf, or even kill plants. Because of recent environmental laws, many mining companies now release much less sulfur dioxide than in the past.

Reclaiming damaged areas

"Before I can grow anything on a tailing dump," Ellen explains, "I have to stabilize what's there. If a lot of dust is blowing around, we spray the tailings with a mixture of resin and water. [Resin is a sticky gum that comes from evergreen trees.] The resin forms a hard crust that stops the fine particles from blowing away. The crust doesn't prevent plants from growing.

"Sometimes, we spread chopped straw on the tailings and work it into the surface with a farm machine called a disc. Besides keeping the dust from blowing around, the straw acts as a mulch. It keeps moisture in the soil. As the straw rots, it provides nutrients that the plants need as they grow."

Preparations for planting

"Because tailings are crushed rock, they can be very acidic and don't contain the nutrients that plants need. So we start by spreading ground-up limestone to reduce the high acid content," notes Ellen.

"Seeding is done in late July or early August, when the area is warm and moist. We add slow-release fertilizers to the seeds. We test the soil on a regular basis, and add more limestone and fertilizer, as needed."

Ellen plants each reclaimed area with a mixture of grass and clover. Grass helps hold the soil together, while clover adds nutrients to the soil. As a result, seeds blowing in from nearby areas can grow. After several years, the soil is fertile enough to plant red pine and jack pine. When these trees grow to maturity, the area will be a forest again.

"I supervise two full-time and 51 seasonal employees," Ellen remarks. "In the last 10 years, these people have planted over 200 000 tree seedlings on tailings. Happily, as many as 90 percent of the trees have survived."

Before and after photographs of the results of reclamation efforts in the tailings area. "That's what I like about my job," Ellen says. "I can see that I'm accomplishing something."

All in a day's work

"My work changes, depending on the day and the season," Ellen notes. "In the summer, my first responsibility each day is to outline the tasks for the summer students. They take samples of the soil, water, and vegetation throughout the area.

"My next stop is the garage complex, where most of the agricultural equipment is stored and repaired. This is where seasonal employees pick up their equipment and supplies. I check to see who is in and out, pick up the time sheets, answer questions about the work to be done, and make contact with the staff who supervise daily operations.

"By midmorning, I'm at my desk in the main engineering building. How I spend the rest of my day depends on the time of year. I like being out in the field to check job progress, supervise staff, make a shopping list for spring planting, or evaluate land for future projects. Sometimes, though, I spend the whole day in meetings. That's important, too, because in meetings the mining company finds out how its activities will affect the environment. And the company gets feedback about my reclamation efforts."

Busy all year

"My department never has a slow season," Ellen comments. "In fact, I have a hard time taking holidays. Before one season is wrapped up, I'm already starting to think about the next. Spring, for example, is planning and planting time. We undertake landscaping and reclamation work during the summer. Fall is the time to prepare the soil for the next spring's growing season. And, strange as it may seem, we grow tree seedlings in winter."

Since 1984, the mining company that employs Ellen has grown its own tree seedlings in unused mine shafts. "The deeper the shaft, the warmer the temperature remains year-round," Ellen explains. "At 1400 m deep, the

Tree seedlings are planted in biodegradable paper pots, grown under artificial lights, and automatically watered and fertilized — all at 1400 m underground!

It's a Fact

Ellen plants a lot of alfalfa and trefoil because these plants can turn nitrogen gas from the air into a nitrogen fertilizer. As the plants die, they rot and add this fertilizer to the soil.

Ellen is holding some pine seedlings that grew underground for 16 weeks. When brought to the surface, the seedlings are "hardened off" for two weeks before planting. ("Hardening off" means allowing the plants to get used to natural sunlight and surface temperatures.) The structure above Ellen's head protects the seedlings from direct sunlight.

Seasonal employees plant seedlings in the tailings area.

rock is a constant 24°C. This is an ideal temperature for growing tree seedlings. I find it exciting to see the plants grow underground — especially when it's cold and snowy up on the surface."

Public relations

As part of her job, Ellen also deals with the public. "I sometimes get a complaint that a piece of mining equipment has run over someone's property. Then there are people who wonder about a strange yellow dust on their cars — they think it came from our sulfur emissions. And there are always calls from students working on Science Fair projects.

"I try to handle each question individually. I investigate to see whether the company's equipment actually did damage someone's property. If it did, I arrange for the property to be repaired.

"The yellow dust is easy to explain. The town where I work is surrounded by large wilderness areas with many different kinds of trees and other plants. In spring and early summer, these plants release large amounts of pollen. We get so much pollen that it can actually cover cars.

"To help the students who contact me, I send them information about my company's reclamation program. When I have time, I also judge Science Fairs. I am amazed by some of the students' ideas!"

Activity

Which grows best?

Ellen spends a lot of time preparing the mine tailings so that plants can grow on them. Why is this necessary? See for yourself by growing plants in fine sand and in potting soil.

You will need

2 flower pots of identical size, with a hole in the bottom of each one
enough potting soil to fill one pot
enough fine sand to fill one pot
2 shallow trays
8 bean seeds

Procedure

1. Place each pot on a shallow tray. Fill one pot with the potting soil and the second with the sand. Examine the two soils. How are they different?
2. Test the soils' ability to hold water. Pour the same amount of water over each soil. Which one holds more water?

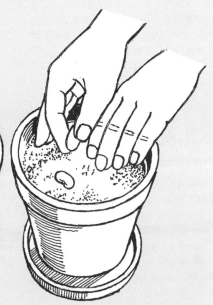

3. Plant 4 bean seeds in each pot. Place the pots near a window. Add water when the soil feels dry to the touch.
4. Examine the plants daily, and record what happens in each pot.
5. After you've done this experiment, make some changes and try it again. For example, you might add lime, fertilizer, compost, or mulch to the pots. Experiment with different items and combinations.

How to become an environmental horticulturist

Ellen has always been interested in growing things. "In high school, I studied biology, chemistry, and physics. I didn't know what I wanted to be. But I knew I wanted to be involved with science and the outdoors," she explains. "So the college course that interested me most was a hands-on horticultural course.

"It's hard to believe now, but back in those days, women weren't allowed to enroll in the course. Horticulture was considered a job for males only. I didn't agree, so I took the next best thing: a degree program in environmental horticulture. This program included studying how to use shrubs and flowers to help the environment. I also learned about using farm crops to improve soils."

As mining areas are reclaimed, the first plants to gain a foothold are grasses. Ellen also likes to use plants such as bird's foot trefoil — the yellow flower in the center of this photograph. This plant adds nutrients to the soil.

Summer field work

"While I was at college," Ellen recalls, "I worked during the summer for the agriculture department of a large mining company." Most of the work involved planting trees and taking care of plants.

"I worked hard. My supervisors must have noticed my efforts, because the company offered me a full-time job when I graduated. At the time, I thought I would work at reclamation for a couple of years, then look for something else. But this job is so rewarding that I've been here for 16 years."

Is this career for you?

Environmental horticulturists spend a lot of time working on their own. This means they must be self-starters. "In order to supervise other workers, you have to be able to work without supervision yourself," Ellen says. "It's also important to be able to work cooperatively. Most of the work is done by crews of about 10 people. The best crew members are good team workers. When they see that something needs to be done, they just go ahead and accomplish it.

"You must also be able to express yourself well," she says. "This is important when explaining reclamation projects to the company's managers. Expressing yourself well is also necessary when dealing with the public. And I often write reports for the company and letters to students."

Ellen is extremely safety-conscious. "Everyone has to be careful. When I'm exploring rough terrain, I always wear safety boots. On worksites, I check to make sure employees are wearing safety boots, hard hats, and protective glasses."

Learn basic math

Although a science background is important for this job, skill in advanced mathematics is not. "Some people think that all science-related jobs require people who are good in mathematics. This isn't necessarily true," Ellen points out. "It is important to learn basic mathematics. But don't be overly concerned if you're not good at advanced math. If I need to figure out some statistics, for example, I simply hire an expert statistician."

Career planning

Volunteer to plant trees for an environmental or conservation group. Keep a journal in which you describe how you feel about what you're doing.

Making Career Connections

Interview a farmer to find out more about crop management. What techniques can reduce soil erosion?

Write to the environmental coordinator of a large company. What environmental issues particularly concern this person? What is being done to tackle these issues?

Write to a college or an association to request information about becoming an environmental horticulturist. A guidance counselor or librarian can help you locate addresses in directories.

Getting started

Interested in being an environmental horticulturist? Here's what you can do now.

1. Read magazines that discuss the environment. Learn about issues such as acid rain and wetlands reclamation.
2. As a summer job, cut lawns and do gardening for your neighbors. Learn how to operate and do simple repairs on lawn mowers.
3. Experiment with plants by growing them in different ways.
4. Join a community group or a public speaking group. Participate in public activities and functions. This will give you experience in talking to groups.
5. If you can, join Junior Farmers, 4-H, or another agricultural or horticultural organization.
6. In high school, plan to take English, computer science, and a variety of science courses, including chemistry and biology.

Related careers

Here are some related careers you may want to check out.

Plant pathologist
Studies plant diseases and pests. Investigates what is causing growth problems, and suggests solutions to those problems. Often works for environmental or agricultural companies or government departments. May also do research at a college.

Greenhouse worker
Responsible for growing plants for commercial markets. Plants include tropical species, flowers, bedding plants, forestry seedlings, and many others. Must have knowledge of plant care and requirements, as well as knowledge of greenhouse operation.

Park maintenance worker
Maintains the grass and gardens in public parks. Fertilizes plants, and adds mulch when needed. Must recognize insect pests and plant diseases.

Future watch

Because of a worldwide concern for the environment, the profession of environmental horticulture will continue to grow. Mining companies, logging companies, chemical companies, and large manufacturers are all interested in land reclamation. Expect opportunities in private, government, and international agencies. Experience gained can often be transferred to work abroad.

Wilderness Outfitters

PERSONAL PROFILE

Career: Wilderness outfitters, kayaking instructors, and tour guides. Tim: "We show people how to appreciate the outdoors in their daily lives."

Interests: Cross-country skiing. "During the summer, we have no time for anything but our business. We belong to several environmental and outdoor clubs, and have two children through the Foster Parents Plan."

Latest accomplishment: Kathy recently started a Waste Crisis Group that is urging the local government to find ways to reduce garbage.

Why we do what we do: "We love being outdoors."

I am: Tim: A problem-solver, a detail-checker, someone who keeps things going. Kathy: Outgoing, people-oriented, likes working with numbers. "The combination of these traits is what makes our business successful."

What I wanted to be when I was in school: Kathy: "A secretary or a travel agent." Tim: "I don't remember wanting to be anything specific. Participation in an out-trip club showed me I wanted to work outdoors."

What a wilderness outfitter does

Kathy and Tim Dyer own a paddling center and wilderness shop. They teach people how to paddle kayaks and canoes, they guide kayak and canoe trips, and they sell a variety of outdoor gear.

Throughout the summer, their business offers half-day courses in kayaking for beginners. They also teach more advanced techniques, such as how to roll a kayak without falling out. In May and June, they give one- and two-day courses in kayak rescue and canoe certification. During July and August, the Dyers and their staff lead a four-day kayak trip each week.

The Dyers' store carries a wide variety of outdoor equipment: tents, kayaks, canoes, clothing, and camping gear. "We try to balance high quality with prices our clients can afford," Tim comments.

It's all part of the job

The Dyers' business is a result of personal dreams and their commitment to the environment. However, Tim admits, "We have to make money, just like any other business."

"To market our services," Kathy explains, "we develop ads for magazines, newspapers, and radio. We've designed a brochure to send to prospective clients and to display at

Tim shows a student how to hold the kayak paddle so that the blades are at right angles to the water.

outdoor shows. And we provide slide shows and demonstrations for many clubs and parks."

In addition, the Dyers answer many telephone queries. "Promotion requires a lot of office time," Tim says. "However, many of the people who start as customers become our friends."

Planning pays off

Although they spend a lot of time in their shop, the Dyers' hearts are with their wilderness trips. "Planning is the hardest part," Tim says, pointing to a stack of menus, equipment lists, and safety checks. "It takes two staff members one full day just to pack the gear!"

"The trip starts when participants meet, introduce themselves, and explain what they want to learn from the trip," Kathy explains. "Next, we teach them how to select gear, how to get in and out of a kayak, and how to paddle. We caution them not to overexert themselves."

Once the group is comfortable handling the boats, the Dyers outline safety procedures. "All of our trip leaders carry complete rescue gear and know how to use it," Tim comments. "All of them understand accident prevention, self-rescue, how to approach and stabilize a rescue victim, and how to treat hypothermia [abnormally low body temperature]."

A student learns the paddle strokes needed to "roll" a kayak — to turn the boat over and right it again. Rolling is a method of self-rescue in case the kayak flips. Otherwise, you must get out of the kayak under water, turn the kayak right-side-up, and climb back in. The Inuit, who invented the kayak, learned to roll their kayaks because Arctic waters are so cold.

All in a day's work

Winter days are slow, giving the Dyers time to plan their business promotions and visit friends. Summertime is busy, consisting of trip days and teaching days. In the summer, the shop is open for business every day.

On a wilderness trip

While out on a trip, the Dyers wake up in their tent early in the morning. They make coffee and awaken their clients. Everyone works together to prepare breakfast on a propane stove. "When they're kayaking, people need a good breakfast that will provide a lot of energy," says Tim.

After breakfast, part of the group packs up the tents. Others make sandwiches for lunch and wash the breakfast dishes. "The garbage detail washes and crushes the cans," Kathy notes. "They're carried home to be recycled." The Dyers promote the idea of "taking nothing but pictures and leaving nothing but footprints." After listening to the weather forecast on a portable radio, Kathy and Tim review the day's route with the group and paddle off down the lake.

It's a Fact

A lightweight tent that packs in a small bag is ideal for the type of camping that the Dyers do. Practice setting up the tent before you leave on your trip!

"By canoeing or kayaking, we're able to see areas that are otherwise very difficult to explore," says Kathy.

A flotilla of kayaks

On the water, one leader is always in the front boat and a second leader brings up the rear. The kayakers paddle within talking distance of each other. At noon, the group stops for lunch, a swim or a nap, or more practice in kayaking skills. "We're soon on the water again," Kathy comments. "We stop at about 4 o'clock to set up camp."

Kathy warns clients about problems to watch for while on the water: dehydration, sun exposure, and heat exhaustion. "When you're paddling a kayak," she explains, "you sweat because of the heat and exercise, so you need to drink a lot of water. You may not realize you're sweating, because the breeze keeps you cool."

"You can get a sunburn much more quickly on water than on land," Tim adds. "The sun's rays bounce off the water and strike your skin

indirectly. You should wear a hat and use a sunscreen with a protection factor of at least 25."

Kathy shows a tent to a customer. The backyard of the Dyers' store is filled with tents of all shapes and sizes.

Setting up camp

When the kayakers arrive at a campsite for the night, they pitch their tents, then swim or relax before preparing supper. "On the first evening, we have meat with our supper," explains Tim. "After that, we prepare vegetarian meals, because vegetable protein keeps without refrigeration.

"Our last job of the night is to pull the boats far enough out of the water to avoid damage by wind and rain," says Tim. "We pack the food inside the kayaks to reduce smells that might attract animals."

A day in the shop

The Dyers' store usually opens at 9:00 a.m., but on a teaching day the students arrive at 8:00 a.m. "If it's not a teaching day," Tim explains, "we check the rental bookings and prepare the boats for the clients."

The Dyers and their staff then serve customers, repair boats, and clean the store. One person handles correspondence, bills, and rental bookings. "Not a day goes by that somebody doesn't say, 'What a lovely life you have!'" Tim laughs. "They only see the interesting parts."

Food in the wilderness

Besides eating nutritious meals, most outdoor enthusiasts carry little bags of "GORP" to supply energy quickly. GORP — Good Old Raisins and Peanuts — contains nuts, raisins, seeds, dates, banana chips, and chocolate chips.

Activity

Plan a wilderness trip

Imagine that you and some friends are going on a kayak trip in the wilderness for two days and one night. Plan your trip using the following questions as guidelines.

1. How would you get information about the wilderness area? What kind of information would you seek?
2. Make a list of all the equipment you would need. Would you rent it, buy it, or borrow it?
3. Whom would you tell about your route and your travel plans? Why would you need to tell someone?
4. List the safety precautions you would take.
5. What would you take to help you find your route?
6. What sort of place would you choose as a campsite?
7. Plan your menu for the trip. List all the food you would need, including the amounts.
8. What would you do with your garbage?

You need maps like this one when you're on a wilderness trip in an area you don't know very well. The map shows details such as buildings, contours, and roads.

How to become a wilderness outfitter

Kathy and Tim met at college, where Kathy studied geography and Tim took environmental studies. After they graduated, they both became teachers. They soon realized that they wanted an outdoor business located in a small town, near water, and within driving distance of their families. After saving their money for several years, they bought a piece of property on a small lake near one of the Great Lakes.

"We started small," Kathy recalls. "We invested in some equipment, converted our vehicle so it could carry what we needed, and then remodeled our house to hold part of the store."

During the first five years, the Dyers taught part-time to boost their income. When the business expanded, they built a small shop and began hiring help. "We now employ 10 people, including two student apprentices during the summer months," says Kathy.

Is this career for you?

The Dyers enjoy their business because they can spend a lot of time outdoors. They meet many interesting people. They also feel they're in control of their own lives. And, by having a business at home, they're both able to spend a lot of time with their son, Jesse.

"Our business gives us freedom, but it also ties us down. We are our own bosses. We make the decisions. But we have to be here seven days a week from April to October," Kathy makes a face. "By the end of the summer, we're glad to put the boats away.

"You have to be a risk-taker," Kathy continues. "When we started our business, we didn't know whether it would succeed. We were taking a big chance. Also, you have to be patient. It takes about five years for a business like this to pay off. You have to make sacrifices today for something you want in the future."

One of the Dyers' greatest business strengths is their people skills. Both Kathy and Tim are good listeners, and they are flexible in the way they deal with others. "There are days when I feel frustrated because of the lack of privacy," Kathy admits, pointing to a lunch table covered with sandwich fixings for staff and visitors. "But when we're alone, the place feels empty."

Outdoor enthusiasts spend money on wilderness adventures, such as hiking, white-water rafting, and trail-riding on horseback. Trail rides can range from a half-day jaunt to a week-long camping holiday.

Career planning

"Job shadow" a wilderness store owner or a kayaking instructor. In job shadowing, you ask permission to watch the person at work, and take notes on the tasks they do.

Offer to help out with a wilderness trip or program. Keep a diary of the tasks that are done and how they are done.

Making Career Connections

Talk to people who take their vacations in the wilderness. Find out what they like and dislike about their experiences. Using their responses, write an article on how to have a successful wilderness trip.

Write to a school or an organization to find out how to become a qualified instructor in a recreational activity. Your school guidance counselor or a librarian can help you find addresses of places to contact.

Getting started

Interested in becoming a wilderness outfitter? Here's what you can do now.

1. Join a canoe club or a kayaking club. Take courses on how to handle these boats.
2. Study field guides of local birds, plants, and trees. Learn to identify the common plants and animals in your area.
3. Take swimming and life-saving lessons.
4. Join your school's out-trip club. If there isn't one at your school, start one.
5. Try to get a part-time or summer job working in an outdoor store or at a resort or summer camp.
6. Study science, geography, computer and math courses. And take language courses. Tourists from other countries will appreciate it if you speak to them in their language.

Related careers

Here are some related careers you may want to check out.

Travel agent
Plans trips for people interested in specific areas and events, for example, worldwide tours that highlight environmentally sensitive areas. Often travels abroad to find locations that would interest clients.

Fishing guide
Takes experienced and novice anglers into wilderness areas. Must understand the behavior of fish. Is responsible for the clients' safety.

Tourism coordinator
Many districts, municipalities, and towns hire people who research and advertise local tourist opportunities. Tourism coordinators "sell" these opportunities at business lunches, at outdoor shows, and on radio and TV.

Future watch

People enjoy outdoor recreation. As they become more and more concerned about the environment, they will become more interested in exploring and preserving wilderness areas. International tourists, especially, want to travel into isolated regions. This international market will continue to grow.

Linda Söber

Environmental Biologist

PERSONAL PROFILE

Career: Environmental biologist. "I run an environmental consulting company. I assess the plants and the animals in an area. This information helps the landowner use the land without harming the natural environment."

Interests: Art, home renovation, and coaching gymnastics. "I like to sketch things in the bush. When I get home, I do watercolors based on my sketches."

Latest accomplishment: Helped design a nature trail highlighting some unique plants and a beaver dam.

Why I do what I do: "I want to help people find ways to use land without harming the environment."

I am: Obsessive, full of energy, enthusiastic, and talkative. "I think I talk too much sometimes. But I get excited about things — especially about the outdoors and the environment."

What I wanted to be when I was in school: "A doctor. But then I realized that I would worry too much if a patient died."

What an environmental biologist does

Environmental biologists study living things and their relationships with other living things around them. "People hire me to find out what plants and animals live on their land," Linda Söber explains. "My work involves exploring swamps, fields, and forests at different times of day. I count each type of plant and animal I see. Once I know what's there, I can help the owners and developers find ways to protect the natural environment."

Protecting the environment

"About 65 percent of my job involves checking areas such as shorefronts and swamps," says Linda. "Building docks along a lakeshore can kill water plants, so that fish have nowhere to lay their eggs. Building on swamps requires filling them in. This destroys the swamps, which have more wildlife than fields or forests. Sometimes I find a high piece of ground where people can build without damaging the surroundings.

"Sometimes clients want me to tell them that nothing will interfere with their plans," Linda comments. "But I can't always do that. If the piece of property is the habitat of a plant or animal that is endangered, I have to tell the client.

"I like working with people who want to use land without harming it. For example, developers can protect rare salamanders by building houses away from the water. Also, building farther back makes the river or lake more attractive. In the long run, such lots are worth more money."

Planning parks is fun

"The government sometimes hires me to assess an area where it plans to put a park," Linda remarks. "Once I know what lives in the area, I help develop the plan for the park. I often suggest that no all-terrain vehicles be allowed along a sandy beach where rare plants are growing."

Extinct, endangered, or rare?

Extinct plants and animals no longer exist. Dinosaurs, saber-toothed tigers, and dodo birds are all extinct.

Endangered species still exist, but their numbers are low and may be declining. In 1941, only 22 whooping cranes were left in the wild. Now, thanks to a recovery plan involving Canadian and American conservation workers, more than 200 of these cranes survive. But the large, white water birds are still considered endangered.

Rare species may be low in numbers in one area, but have a healthy population elsewhere. Sugar maple trees, for example, are rare on the northwest coast of North America, but are common in the east.

Indoor tasks

Once Linda explores an area, she writes a report explaining what she has seen. "One report was really exciting to write," she recalls, "because I had found an endangered eagle.

"Because I'm self-employed and my business is new, I do a lot of things myself. Each month, for example, I spread out my accounts on the kitchen table. I also handle all my own letter-writing and advertising. When I'm more established, I hope to hire someone else to do these things for me.

"Once a month," says Linda, "I call a list of people who might need to hire a firm like mine. These people include government officials, land planning agencies, lawyers, and engineers."

"When I'm exploring forests, fields, and swamps, I never know what I'm going to find," Linda notes. "Last year, I almost stepped on a nest of young marsh hawks. I try to walk as carefully as possible, of course, so that I don't disturb what's living there."

All in a day's work

"Because different animals are active at different times of day, my schedule revolves around the species I'm trying to identify," comments Linda. "If I'm assessing morning birds, I'm up at 5 a.m. to be on site by 6:30. Starlings and swallows are easier to identify in the evening, when they come into a marsh to roost. They fly so close you can almost reach up and touch them.

"Other birds are so shy you rarely see them. Virginia rails hide in cattails. But during breeding season, they answer recorded bird calls. But I'm careful not to keep playing the call, or I might scare the female off her nest."

Nature — the best teacher

"Nature teaches me something new every day. When I first looked for young salamanders, I read that they are found along the edges of boggy areas. It took a lot of looking before I found the right kind of place to check."

It's a Fact

Dead trees are full of life! As the trees rot, birds such as bluebirds and woodpeckers use holes in the trunks for their nests, insects eat the rotten wood and provide food for the birds, and bracket fungus grows on the trunks.

The "S" method of identifying animals

Sight: Looking closely at an animal's size, shape, color, and other features can help you identify it.

Sign: Are there tracks, feces, bedding sites, or nests? Deer and rabbits are often identified by their oval feces.

Sound: Morning and evening are the best times to identify sounds, but sounds can be confusing. Some frogs, for example, sound like birds. "One spring, I heard what sounded like 400 ducks," Linda laughs. "I tried to sneak up on them, and found that the 'ducks' were frogs!"

Identifying animals can be tricky

The sharp-shinned hawk and the cooper's hawk have similar coloring, but the sharp-shinned hawk is a little smaller. Since female hawks are larger than male hawks, a female sharp-shinned hawk could be mistaken for a small male cooper's hawk. You can tell the two apart by examining their tails. The sharp-shinned hawk has a squared-off tail, while the tail of the cooper's hawk is round.

A cooper's hawk.   A sharp-shinned hawk.

Changes with the season

"In the early spring, I search for pike eggs at the base of cattails in a swamp. If I find them, I know that draining that swamp would kill the pikes' eggs, resulting in fewer fish in a nearby lake.

"In the fall, birds flying south land in the marshes. We need to preserve the marshes so that these birds will have enough to eat during their migration."

Office work

Linda spends 60 percent of her time outdoors, and 40 percent in her office at home. "This part of my job is more predictable," says Linda. "Tasks such as inputting all my field notes on the computer are boring. But I learn so much from these notes."

Looking for snakes

Woodpiles are good hiding places for snakes. Linda carefully lifts a bottom log to see what's underneath. "I often see a milk snake sunning itself on a rock near this woodpile," she says. Since snakes are reptiles, their body temperatures change with the surrounding temperatures. Lying in the sun speeds up their body processes and helps them digest their food.

Activity

What's there?

To get an idea of the type of work Linda Söber does, try your own plant and animal assessment.

You will need
string
sketch pad
notebook
calculator
guides to local plants and animals

Procedure
1. Take a walk in a local park or conservation area.
2. With string, mark off an area 20 cm square on a grassy part of the park, or 1 m square in a forested area.
3. Sketch every kind of plant and animal you find in that area.
4. Count the numbers of individuals of each kind of living thing that you find inside the square.
5. Use guidebooks to help you identify each species.
6. Which animal or plant did you find most frequently in your square? What was its population (that is, how many individuals were there in the square)?
7. Calculate the total area of the field or forest in which you are working. For the animal or plant that was most common in your square, calculate how many individuals of that species might live in the park.

If you found five dandelions in your 20 cm X 20 cm square, there might be about 125 dandelions in a 1 m square!

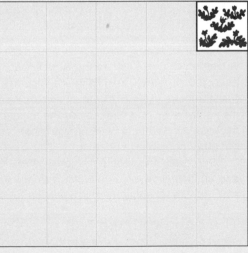

How to become an environmental biologist

After high school, Linda studied biology for four years in college. "But you cannot learn everything from books," she notes. "You also have to spend time with someone who is knowledgeable in the field."

Before starting her own business, Linda worked as a fisheries biologist for a government agency. "I learned a lot from another fisheries biologist. Just watching the way this person handled live fish was an important lesson in conservation.

"I liked working for the government, but every time I was promoted, I spent less time in the field. I finally realized that the next step was district supervisor, and I'd be supervising staff and assigning budgets. I realized I'd rather work outside."

Assess your strengths

"I was thinking about starting my own business when I was assigned to work on a special government project," Linda recalls. "As part of

Linda found these five different grasses in one habitat. Because there are hundreds of different grasses, they are hard to identify in the field. Linda collects samples of any plants she doesn't recognize. She also collects any dead animals she finds. "Once I wrapped a brown bat in freezer paper and dropped it in the freezer. My husband thought it was sausage," Linda laughs.

the project, I checked the assessments other people had done, and I saw that there was a need for people to do these assessments. A lot of people know how to identify species. Other people know how to protect swamps, lakes, and forests. I felt I could do both.

"My partner on the government project was an engineer for a large power company. He knew a lot about plants. So, we teamed up to work together. I line up the clients, and do most of the field work and the animal assessments. He oversees the plant work when I need his expertise."

Is this career for you?

"When I'm canoeing across a swamp in the moonlight, writing down the names of the birds I hear, it's hard to believe that people are paying me to do this," Linda grins. "But they are. I love it because I love being outdoors, but it's not for everyone. Sometimes the mosquitoes are so thick you're breathing them up your nose. I don't mind, but other people might hate it.

"One great thing about this job is learning about plants and animals. I observe them in their natural environment and I read a lot about them in scientific journals."

The good with the bad
"Starting a business was easier than I thought. I showed a profit at the end of my first summer! But the winters are

really slow. I save part of my summer income to pay my winter bills. I enjoy running my own business. I can set my own hours and work around my family's needs. One Sunday, for example, I assessed a marsh that was a two-hour drive from my home. My husband took care of our baby. I left in the midafternoon, watched the moon rise while I listened for evening bird calls, and was home by midnight. That was a day's work.

"Running a business from my house does have its disadvantages, though. At first, my friends and family thought I had time every day to chat on the telephone. I had to make them understand that they shouldn't call me during the day — I have too many tasks to do!"

Career planning

Interview an environmental biologist. What does the job involve? Ask about ways to learn to identify plants and animals.

Making Career Connections

Volunteer to spend a day with a local biologist. Keep a photo diary of your activities.

Take pictures of three different plants and animals. Make notes on how to identify them. Teach a friend how to find and recognize these plants and animals.

With the help of your guidance counselor or a librarian, contact an environmental organization and ask for the name and address of a local member.

Getting started

Interested in being an environmental biologist? Here's what you can do now.

1. Take time to explore the outdoors. What species of plants and animals can you identify? Try to find one new plant and animal species each time you take a walk.
2. Borrow a pair of binoculars. Experiment until you can focus quickly on distant animals.
3. Practice using simple field guides. Once you can identify some common species, start using more advanced guidebooks.
4. Attend a summer wilderness camp.
5. In high school, take biology courses. Chemistry and computer courses are also important. Learn general business skills, too, in case you set up your own office.

Related careers

Here are some related careers you may want to check out.

Botanist
Studies plants and how they grow. Some botanists breed plants to produce better crops or more brightly colored flowers. Some work for drug companies, analyzing different plants to find substances that can be used to fight disease.

Environmental planner
Gathers information from people like Linda Söber, to help determine what areas need protection. Has knowledge of government regulations and statutes regarding land use.

Outdoor writer
Writes books, articles, and scripts about the outdoors. Many outdoor writers specialize in topics such as fishing, plant identification, environmental issues, and education.

Future watch

As more people realize that their activities have an impact on the environment, the field of environmental biology will expand. Industries are also becoming more concerned about the environment, and will hire more people with skills like Linda's. "Monitoring what is happening now will help us avoid problems in the future," Linda states.

Michelle Martin

Park Naturalist

PERSONAL PROFILE

Career: Park naturalist. "I lead programs that help people get to know and appreciate the outdoors."

Interests: Acrylic painting, swimming, playing guitar, and singing. "I wrote some environmental songs that I use in my work."

Latest accomplishment: Volunteer work at a school for the hearing-impaired, and use of sign language in her everyday work. "When I talk to students about an animal, I teach them how to say the animal's name in sign language. The kids love it."

Why I do what I do: "When I was growing up, I loved learning about wild plants and animals. I also enjoyed backpacking, river-rafting, and bike-hiking. In this job, I get paid to do things I love to do."

I am: Outgoing, adventurous, creative. "I like to think of interesting ways to teach. For example, I use music to help young children learn about how a tree grows."

What I wanted to be when I was in school: "A doctor, because I wanted to help people."

What a park naturalist does

Two hundred years ago, most settlers in North America lived in rural areas. They shared their farm fields with snakes and mice. Bats lived under the eaves of their log cabins. Birds sang from the nearby trees. Because the settlers lived among animals, they learned a lot about them.

Today, most of us live in cities. We don't see bats or snakes. Often, we don't even hear birds — their songs are drowned out by traffic noise. Because many North Americans don't know much about the outdoors, they sometimes don't appreciate its importance.

As a park naturalist, Michelle Martin works to change this attitude. "I plan educational programs for elementary and high school students, teachers, conservation groups, and the general public," she explains. "My programs include nature walks, forest studies, and birdwatching. Once people start to enjoy nature, they want to learn more about it," notes Michelle. "Part of my job is to answer many different questions about the natural environment."

Early adventures

"When I was a teenager, I was an avid Girl Scout," Michelle recalls. "I loved scouting because I could spend a lot of time outdoors. I guess I've never outgrown that desire.

"One summer, I went on a Girl Scout expedition. We took courses on how to survive in the wild. Then we were left on an isolated island with no food. If we wanted food, we had to catch it or pick it ourselves."

First encounters with snakes

Michelle has noticed that a lot of people are afraid of snakes. However, she sees that many people change their minds about snakes and other reptiles when they get to know them better. "I run a Nature Center full of snakes, lizards, and turtles," she explains. "People can handle the snakes while we discuss their importance in nature.

"You may find it hard to believe, but snakes actually have distinct personalities. Once, when I was showing reptiles to a group of 9-year-olds, one of the boys showed me a corn snake that had somehow got into an empty turtle cage. I don't know where the snake came from, but when I tried to pick it up, it was tame enough to handle.

"Teaching people about snakes is a challenge," Michelle admits. "A few months ago, a park visitor killed a snake he thought was a water moccasin. He said it *had* to be a water moccasin because it was swimming in the lake. It was actually a harmless eastern king snake."

Water moccasins vs. king snakes

Some snakes, such as water moccasins and eastern king snakes, may be seen swimming in lakes. The water moccasin or cottonmouth is a venomous (poisonous) snake. The venom paralyzes the small mammals that this type of snake eats. People who are bitten can get very sick, and sometimes die. The eastern king snake is black, with narrow white rings around its body. King snakes eat water moccasins, other snakes, and other small animals.

Roads are a problem for turtles. During the spring, they search for warm, dry places to lay their eggs. Many of the best places are beside roads. If only there were turtle-crossing areas!

All in a day's work

Michelle gets up early, and walks her two dogs before breakfast. "I arrive at my office by 8 o'clock. From then on, I rarely do the same thing two days in a row.

"First, I feed the Nature Center animals and clean their cages. The number and variety of these animals change constantly. I always have some snakes, turtles, and lizards, but I don't like caging animals that live in the wild. Instead, I keep them for a couple of weeks, use them to show park visitors, and then release them."

School programs

"For school groups, my favorite activities are simulation games," says Michelle. "The students pretend to be wild animals, to learn what happens in the wild. For example, in 'Run Rabbit Run,' each student is given one of three different-colored tags. One color is for foxes, another color for rabbits, and the third is for voles, which are very small, mouselike animals.

"At the end of the game, students discuss what it might be like to be one of these animals. Some get really angry when a fox catches them because they were stopping to catch their breath. But that's the way it is in nature," Michelle observes.

"When older students play the game, I add humans such as a hunter and a naturalist. If the hunter 'shoots' a lot of rabbits, the foxes may not find enough food for their pups. On the other hand, too many rabbits can damage the environment."

These students are touching a snake for the first time. Michelle thinks that if people learn about snakes, they won't want to harm them.

It's a Fact

An incredible number of plants and insects have never been identified. Many of these organisms live in the rain forests of South America or Southeast Asia.

A tricky dilemma

This woman raises orphaned raccoons. When they're old enough, she releases them into the wild. But what should she do with a blind raccoon, a three-legged deer, or an eagle with only one wing? Should wild animals be kept in cages so that humans can learn about them? Many naturalists like Michelle struggle with this question. What would you do?

Summer programs

During the summer, school programs are replaced by day camps and day-care programs. "I enjoy introducing preschool children to the natural world. I often start by giving each of them a crayon. I challenge them to find a wild flower or a leaf in the same color. Afterwards, we discuss why plants and animals have the colors they do."

Michelle also supervises about 15 student volunteers between the ages of 11 and 16. "I couldn't get along without them," she comments. "They catch fish for the aquarium in the Nature Center, and they find snakes, toads, and lizards for the Center as well. They also inform visitors about upcoming programs."

Encouraging action

Michelle also encourages people to do something to improve their own environment. "Many people know that black rhinoceroses, giraffes, and rain forests are endangered," she says. "But they don't realize that there are endangered plants and animals close to their homes, as well. Some live right here in the park."

Poaching: A serious crime

Each year, poachers kill thousands of black bears. All they want are the gall bladders and claws, which are cut out and sold to make medicines. This illegal trade is threatening bear populations throughout the world.

When she isn't working with students, visitors, or volunteers, Michelle prepares press releases and talks to the media. "This is important because people can't attend the park programs if they don't hear about them."

Some species, like the trumpeter swan, are making a comeback.

Activity

What's in the pond?

In order to learn about animals, you must observe them in their natural habitats. Ponds are the easiest places to find a variety of animals. Be sure to get permission to go to the pond, and be careful when working at the pond's edge.

You will need

clothes hanger
broom handle
wire cutters
electric tape
old nylon stocking
stapler
flat pan, e.g., a light-colored plastic
    dishpan
tweezers
nature guidebooks from the library or
    a bookstore

Procedure

1. Cut the clothes hanger, as shown in the diagram.

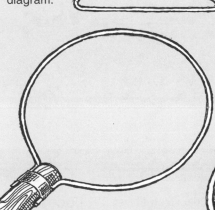

2. Form it into a loop. Use electric tape to attach the wire loop tightly to one end of the broom handle.
3. Stretch the nylon stocking over the wire loop. Staple the nylon in place.

4. Using this net, dip material from the bottom of a pond or stream.
5. Pour the material into a flat pan. Add a little water from the pond. Carefully examine the material, as you move things around with the tweezers. Use nature guides to help you identify what you find.

How to become a park naturalist

In high school, Michelle studied biology, chemistry, and physics. After high school, she earned degrees in English literature and in outdoor teacher education. "I like to learn, so I'm now studying French by correspondence and taking a botany course at a local college," she says.

According to Michelle, park naturalists come from a variety of backgrounds. "Naturalists don't always have advanced science degrees," she explains. "Many are historians, hikers, storytellers, or musicians. They all have two things in common, though. They love being outdoors, and they enjoy working with people."

Communication is important

"In my job, it's very important to be able to talk to people," Michelle points out. "I work with people of all ages. I simplify things for very young children, but I also have to answer hard questions from students and older people."

Of course, Michelle can't answer every question she is asked. "If I don't know the answer, I say so," she admits. "Sometimes I offer to find the answer and get back to the person later. At other times, students find the answer and let me know. That's why I like working with young people. They ask a lot of good questions and they don't mind doing research to find the answers."

Many historic sites hire students in the summer to reenact scenes of daily life in the past. These outdoor jobs often require a knowledge of history and languages, and an interest in acting.

It's a Fact

In one night, a bat can eat 500 insects!

Is this career for you?

"One thing I like about this job is that nature always has something new to teach me. I can never know it all because nature is always changing.

"In my work, I try to be organized, because I plan and carry out all of the programs at the park. I also set up workshops in elementary schools. I have to make sure that I have the right materials, in the right place, in order to run each program."

Fact and fiction

"I often use literature in my teaching," Michelle says. "Have you ever noticed, for example, how bats are portrayed in children's stories? They're often shown as scary, bloodsucking vampires. When I talk about bats, I tell people how useful they are. For example, they keep insect populations under control."

Career planning

Interview a park naturalist about the endangered plants and animals in a local park. Make a display explaining what people can do to help protect these plants and animals.

Making Career Connections

Interview people with hearing loss or other physical challenges. Find out what difficulties they have in enjoying nature, and how they overcome these difficulties.

Park naturalists must often caution visitors who harm animals or plants. Role-play how you might talk to a park visitor whom you found cutting branches from a tree.

Volunteer to help out at a local park. What jobs do volunteers do? Try to learn about as many different jobs as you can.

Getting started

Interested in being a park naturalist? Here's what you can do now.

1. Spend a lot of time outdoors. Sit quietly in a natural setting. Listen to the sounds around you. Try to identify what you hear.
2. Participate in organizations such as Girl Scouts, Girl Guides, Boy Scouts, Rangers, and nature clubs that teach useful outdoor skills.
3. Join a public speaking club. Practice speaking in front of a group.
4. Go on a "camera hunt." Shoot nothing but pictures. How close can you get to the animals?
5. Use field guides to help you identify trees, wild flowers, and insects. Label your photographs with the names of the animals and plants.
6. In high school, take courses in biology, botany, outdoor education, media literacy, and communications. Don't forget physical education — you have to be in good shape to work outdoors.

Related careers

Here are some related careers you may want to check out.

Conservation officer
Enforces wildlife and habitat protection laws, and hunting and fishing regulations. Patrols outdoor recreation areas. Provides information on how game laws protect the environment.

Historical interpreter
Develops and teaches programs at historic sites. May portray a person living in a past era, and perform that person's tasks. Must enjoy role-playing and talking with people of all ages. Many craftspeople, like blacksmiths and weavers, are employed at historic sites.

Outdoor photographer
Photographs animals and plants in their natural environment. Sells these photos to magazines, books, and newspapers. May also shoot videos or films for television production companies.

Future watch

Many people now have more leisure time, and want to spend some of this time outdoors. Also, more people now live in cities, and they don't see wildlife in their daily lives. These social changes, plus increasing concern for the environment, have resulted in more jobs in outdoor education. This trend should continue.

Tom Kudloo

Aerologist

PERSONAL PROFILE

Career: Aerologist. "I collect the information that helps weather forecasters predict North American weather patterns."

Interests: Hunting and fishing. "From the middle of July to the end of August, I run a fishing camp for tourists who fly into the area."

Latest accomplishment: Promotion to weather station manager.

Why I do what I do: "I like technology. This job allows me to work with computers and with the various pieces of equipment used to monitor the weather."

I am: Talkative, friendly, and "quick to throw in a wisecrack."

What I wanted to be when I was in school: "A carpenter or an electrician. When my father worked at a weather office, I asked the technicians all kinds of questions. One day, one of them filled out an application form and suggested that I sign it. I did."

What an aerologist does

Everybody wants to know what the next day's weather will be like. To make this prediction, weather forecasters need a lot of information. In thousands of weather stations across North America, aerologists observe local conditions and provide some of that information.

Tom Kudloo is an aerologist who works at an "upper air station" in the Arctic. "Twice a day I send up a hydrogen-filled weather balloon," Tom says. "I attach weather instruments and a tiny radio transmitter to the balloon. It rises to about 30 km before it bursts. As the balloon goes up, the radio transmitter sends me information about the air masses above me."

This information is fed into a computer inside the weather station. The data are printed out on a long roll of paper as the balloon continues its flight. "I examine the computer printout and translate the pen squiggles into weather information," Tom explains. "When the balloon's flight is over, I send the information I have gathered to forecast offices in several major cities. From there, it is distributed across North America."

Using weather information

"Weather forecasters use an aerologist's data to predict tomorrow's weather," Tom says. "You hear these forecasts on radio and television. For many people, the forecasts can mean the difference between life and death. For instance, pilots need to know wind direction and speed. If they are flying 'into' the wind, they will have to carry more fuel. Weather forecasters also issue 'small craft warnings,' telling boaters when to expect high winds and big waves."

Twice a day on local radio, Tom gives a weather report in his native language, Inuktitut. "During the winter, a blizzard can blow up quickly. The winds gust to more than 100 km/h, and temperatures drop to minus 45. Without shelter, people would quickly die in such conditions. My reports warn them to stay inside."

Snow depth predicts spring runoff

Twice a week in the winter, Tom measures the snow depth and density. "I twist a hollow tube with a saw on the end into the snow, filling the tube," he explains. "When I remove the tube, I have a 'core sample' of snow. Then I melt the snow. The amount of water I get tells me how dense the snow is. Usually 10 cm of snow produce 1 cm of water. If I get more than this, the snow is very dense, and contains more water than usual. My readings help forecasters predict the amount of spring runoff, and the likelihood of spring floods."

How do forecasters predict the weather?

Forecasters first need a "map" of today's weather. The information for this map comes from observers such as Tom, as well as from weather satellites. Then, forecasters compare today's maps with yesterday's maps, and calculate what will happen tomorrow. For example, if a warm tropical air mass is moving across the prairies, they might predict that it will continue moving in the same direction. We usually get rain just ahead of the warm air.

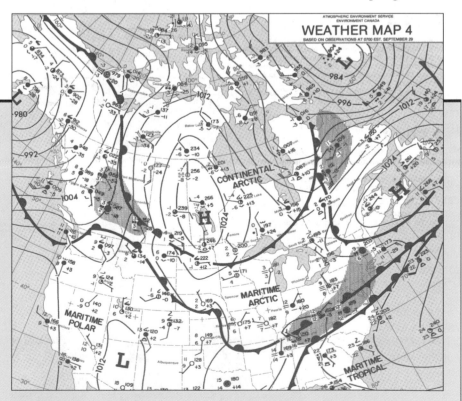

All in a day's work

Tom gets up at 4:00 a.m. each day and arrives at the weather station by around 4:15. "The first part of my job is indoors," Tom explains. "I get the computer ready to record the information that will come from the balloon.

"Then, during the winter, I put on the layers of clothing I need for working outdoors in Arctic temperatures. I wear heavy wool 'long johns' [long underwear]. These are topped by a wool shirt, a heavy sweater, a ski jacket, and a down-filled parka. I also wear wool pants covered by heavily insulated windproof pants. Finally, I wear duffel socks [duffel is a thick coarse wool material], knitted wool socks, and heavily insulated boots."

A hydrogen "lift"

Outside, in a tall garage-like building, Tom checks the machine that makes hydrogen for the weather balloon. The raw material is water, or H_2O, which is made up of hydrogen and oxygen. Running an electric current through water causes the water molecules to break apart, producing hydrogen and oxygen. The oxygen is released to the

Tom's balloon is almost ready. Now he will attach the instruments, take it outside, and send it on its way.

atmosphere, and the hydrogen is stored in large tanks.

Tom attaches the hose from the tank to one of the caramel-colored balloons used to carry the weather instruments aloft. "It takes 20 minutes for the balloon to fill," Tom says. "I watch as it gradually lifts off the table and tugs at the rope that anchors it. When it is almost 2 m in diameter, I check that it will lift a 2 kg weight."

Then Tom attaches the box of instruments. "A cardboard box holds the radio transmitter and a sensor to measure air temperature, air pressure, and humidity. As the balloon rises,

the sensor also measures the balloon's speed and direction. This helps me calculate the wind speed and direction.

"I take the balloon outside and release it at exactly 5:15 a.m. Throughout North America, many other aerologists do exactly the same thing at precisely the same time. Since North America has several time zones, aerologists in other time zones might launch their balloons at, say, 3:15 a.m. or 6:15 a.m., local time. In this way, we get an overall picture of the air masses over North America at one time.

"After I launch the balloon, I go back inside to the computer. By about 9:00 a.m., I've translated all the data and sent it to the main forecast offices. Then I go home."

Winter clothing

Why do people wear several layers of clothing during cold weather? Because each layer has a different job. The one closest to the skin absorbs sweat, which keeps moisture away from the skin and keeps the body warmer. The middle layers hold air close to the skin. Once this air has been warmed by body heat, it will help to keep the body warm. The outer layer blocks wind. This prevents heat from being blown away from the body.

It's a Fact

Hydrogen is lighter than air, so balloons filled with hydrogen rise into the sky.

As the balloon rises, the transmitter sends weather information to Tom's computers. A dish antenna similar to a TV satellite dish picks up the data.

"My second shift begins at 4:15 p.m. That's when I prepare to send up a second weather balloon at 5:15 p.m. By 9:00 p.m., I've translated and sent these data as well.

"We are supposed to send up two balloons every day," Tom adds. "Occasionally, it's so windy or there's such a bad storm that it's not safe. One day, I almost got blown away with the balloon. On another, I couldn't see the road from the windows of my house. Since the road is right out front, I knew it wouldn't be safe to try to get to the weather station."

Activity

Make your own barometer

One measurement that Tom takes is air pressure readings. To understand how these readings are obtained, try the following activity.

You will need
balloon
large juice can with the top
  completely removed
thick elastic band
foam tray, such as a supermarket
  meat tray
scissors
glue
sheet of paper

1. Remove the neck from the balloon.
2. Stretch the balloon over the mouth of the can.
3. Secure the balloon firmly in place with an elastic band. The can will resemble a drum.
4. Cut a 2 cm by 2 cm square of material from the meat tray. Glue it to the center of the balloon. Wait for the glue to dry.

TOP VIEW

Enough overhang to balance other end of pointer until glue dries

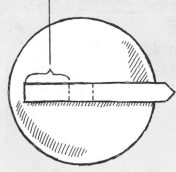

5. Cut a pointer from the meat tray. Glue it to the first piece of foam, as shown in the picture. Make sure that the pointer extends beyond the rim of the can, and that its tip almost touches a piece of paper taped to the wall next to the barometer.
6. Over the period of a week or more, mark any changes in the level of the pointer tip. What is the weather like when the marker rises? What is the weather like when the marker drops?

SIDE VIEW

Base Pointer   Paper taped to wall

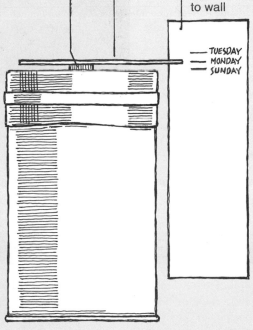

TUESDAY
MONDAY
SUNDAY

7. Why do you think the barometer might work best if you construct it on a cloudy day or a stormy day?

How to become an aerologist

Tom took science, chemistry, and geography courses in high school. "I did miserably in a science course on weather," he recalls. "I told the teacher I didn't care about the weather. I was also lousy in math.

"Even though I wasn't good in these subjects, I tried hard. When I did a science experiment, I was careful to record everything I observed. In geometry, I double-checked every measurement. I was good at geography, though. I had to leave the Arctic in order to attend high school, so I learned a lot about different places.

In his training course, Tom learned how to decipher the signals transmitted by the weather balloon's instruments. "It was like learning a second language, or learning how to crack a code," he recalls.

"And I loved technical studies. I took so many shop courses I could have been a carpenter. My interest in machines and carpentry helps around the weather station. I do all the minor repairs myself."

Government training

Tom's interest in technology and his precision in practical jobs landed him a job with a government weather service. As soon as he was hired, he went on an eight-month training course. "I studied how to observe weather and how to operate weather instruments. I learned how to run and maintain the hydrogen-making equipment. I also practiced filling and releasing weather balloons. The instructors warned us that hydrogen is very dangerous. One little spark can cause it to explode."

Cold air is heavier than warm air. When a cold "arctic" air mass meets a warm "tropical" air mass, the warm air is forced up. As the warm air rises, its moisture condenses to form clouds. This can cause thunder showers during summer months, or snowstorms during the winter.

Is this career for you?

"I feel more comfortable working outdoors than inside, so I like my job," Tom says. "I also have part of my day free to hunt and fish, as long as I'm back to send up the afternoon balloon.

"In a job like this, where my supervisor is a great distance away, I have to be independent," Tom adds. "A lot of the time, I work by myself. As long as I transmit the data at the right time, nobody complains. But if I do run

into trouble, I have to figure out a solution on my own.

"It's important to be precise, to do the same thing at the same time every day," Tom cautions. "I'm also careful when I handle the instruments."

In addition, Tom is a good communicator. "I find it easiest to give the local forecast in Inuktitut. But my English has to be excellent, too, because that's the language of my work."

Career planning

Visit a weather station. Interview aerologists or other weather observers about the work they do. Find out how each person got a start in this career.

Making Career Connections

Spend a day with a local weather forecaster and list the sources of weather information.

Volunteer to help keep a weather watch for your local radio station, television station, or tourist bureau. Keep a journal of your work.

Watch the television weather forecast each day for a week. Keep track of the movement of one particular air mass. What is the weather like just before and just after the air mass passes?

Getting started

Interested in being an aerologist? Here's what you can do now.

1. Take time to observe the weather. Set up a weather station in your backyard or on your apartment balcony. Keep track of the air temperature and wind direction.
2. Observe clouds. Which types bring rain or snow? Which types come with sunny weather?
3. Buy or make a barometer. How does the weather change when the barometer reading goes up? How does it change when the barometer reading goes down?
4. Record the total precipitation (rain, snow, sleet, and hail) your area receives. Use a tin can to collect rain or a ruler to measure snow depth.
5. In high school, study chemistry, physics, and mathematics. Learn to use computers, too, because weather forecasters are becoming more and more dependent on computer data.

Related careers

Here are some related careers you may want to check out.

Meteorological technician
Usually works at a major airport. Informs pilots about the upper air conditions ("winds aloft") and the weather they will encounter during their flights. Often sends weather forecasts to local radio and television stations.

Climatologist
Uses weather data from many years to make generalizations about an area's weather. Studies changes in weather patterns that could indicate global warming.

Hydrology technician
Obtains water samples from rivers and lakes. Measures stream flow. Also measures river and lake levels. Uses this information to predict the amount of spring runoff and the probability of flooding.

Future watch

Weather observation is becoming more and more automated. Radar measures the movement of high air masses, and satellites make temperature and humidity readings. Although weather-related jobs are changing, aerologists, meteorologists (weather forecasters), computer programmers, and electronics technicians will still be in demand in the future.

Charlie Milne — Farmer

The next time you order fries, a hamburger, and a milkshake, think about where this food comes from. Every meal you eat started with a farmer.

"People think you have to grow up in the country to become a farmer," says Charlie Milne. "In fact, that's not true. Farmers are generalists. They have to know about a lot of different things."

Farmers are managers

"As the production manager for a cranberry bog run by a native band, I'm responsible for 20 hectares [43 acres] of cranberry plants," notes Charlie. "We produce about 250 000 kg of cranberries each year. During the fall harvest, I supervise 21 people who help harvest and sell the berries."

Always learning

"I have to know a lot about the crop I'm growing," Charlie comments. "Every year, I take a course to obtain the latest information on cranberry growing. Many other courses are available, too — on everything from making maple syrup and beekeeping, to accounting and how to use computers on a farm."

Concern for the environment

"Because farmers spend so much time outdoors, we care about the environment. For example, I build nesting boxes to attract birds to the cranberry bog to eat insects that might damage the berries. This means I don't have to use as many pesticides.

"Unfortunately, pesticides can kill useful insects like bees, which are necessary for pollination." (In pollination, the pollen from one flower fertilizes a second flower, which leads to the production of seeds and fruits.)

Other skills

"Most farmers need some mechanical know-how," Charlie points out. "It's a lot cheaper and faster to take care of our own trucks, tractors, harvesting equipment, and so on.

"I've also learned some carpentry, because I have to keep my buildings in good repair. Other farmers build animal pens, fences, and barns.

"As you can see," smiles Charlie, "farmers really do know about a lot of different things!"

Charlie Milne runs a cranberry farm. Today, many farmers raise specialty crops, such as kiwi fruit or Chinese ginseng.

This farmer makes some minor adjustments to a piece of machinery. Modern farmers need many different technical skills.

It's a Fact

Some dairy cattle are fed by computer. Each cow wears a collar with an identification tag. When a cow approaches the feeder, a sensor reads the tag and the computer checks to see how much milk the cow gave during the last milking. If the cow gave a lot of milk, she'll need more food.

Getting started

1. Grow a vegetable garden. Learn about the soil, water, and temperature requirements of various plants.
2. Work as a nursery assistant. Find out what insects damage plants. Which insects are helpful?
3. Volunteer as a mechanic's helper. Learn how to maintain gasoline and diesel engines.
4. Work with a carpenter. Learn to use carpentry tools safely.
5. In high school, take courses in botany, chemistry, physics, and computers. Don't forget marketing: many farmers sell their own produce.

Claudia Wilck — Land Surveying Technician

How do construction companies decide where to build a road? How does a power company know the best place to build a dam? How do you know where someone's property ends and someone else's begins? A surveyor can tell you.

"Surveyors measure parcels of land," Claudia Wilck explains. "As a survey technician, I assist the surveyor by operating the surveying instruments and writing down measurements. We work as a team to make sure that the land is measured accurately."

Verifying the location

"Before starting to measure, I have to make sure I'm in the right place," Claudia says. "This is easy in most parts of North America. The whole continent has already been surveyed.

"When surveyors measure a piece of property, they hammer a metal bar into the ground in one corner. If I can't find the bar, I use a metal detector to help me. Then I set up the surveying transit. A transit is a measuring instrument that has a lens similar to a camera lens. It enables me to sight along a straight line. I place the transit on a tripod and make sure it is

level. Then I sight along the line I want to measure.

"If there are branches or small trees in the way, I remove them," Claudia continues. "If a tree is in the way, I survey around it. If I'm careful, I can still get an accurate measurement."

Measuring distance

Early surveyors used metal measuring tapes to check distance. Claudia uses an electronic distance gauge. This instrument sends an electronic beam along the line she is measuring. The beam bounces off a

This highway surveyor uses a transit to check that the roadbed is the correct width.

The plumb line on the bottom of this tripod must hang over the exact spot where the last surveyor left a metal survey bar. Claudia shows a young friend how she checks this.

glass prism at the other end of the line and returns to the measurer. "By figuring out how long it took the beam to go back and forth, the distance gauge can calculate the exact distance of the line," Claudia explains. "It's a lot more accurate than using a measuring tape."

Back at her office, Claudia draws a plan (a type of map) that shows the location and size of the property she has measured. A copy of this plan is registered with the government. It is used to settle any disputes over land ownership.

Getting started

1. Measure the outside perimeter of your house or apartment building. Check your measurements with those taken by two other people. Whose measurement is the most accurate? How do you know?
2. Join an orienteering club. Try following an orienteering course.
3. Visit the local registry office. Check the municipal plan for the lot of the place where you live. Buy a plan of the lot.
4. Interview a surveyor. Ask about the accuracy required in surveying work.
5. At school, take courses in geometry, trigonometry, science, and geography.

Michele Bailey — Civil Engineer

When you zip along on your bicycle, or ride in a car, do you ever think about the road on which you are traveling? Most people don't — unless they are civil engineers.

"Civil engineers like me are responsible for making sure that roads are smooth, safe, and long-lasting," Michele Bailey explains. "My job is to supervise highway and bridge construction, and the development of major intersections."

Paperwork first

"My first task on a project is to check the dozens of blueprint drawings," Michele points out. "Do they show all the information I need? Is a list of necessary materials included? Is the list complete? Then I check all the specifications for the materials that we'll use to build the road. Asphalt and cement must bear a specified amount of weight. The specifications depend on where these materials will be used and how heavily traveled the road will be. Sand, as well, must meet certain specifications. For example, it must contain particles of different sizes. If the sand is too fine, it won't compact properly. These specifications are tested in a laboratory."

Building the road

"Good roads run across well-drained ground," Michele explains. "If we build a road across a swamp, we have to fill it in. To provide a level surface in hilly areas, we dig away some of the higher sections."

Once the ground has been leveled, sand and gravel are laid to form the "roadbed." This is the surface on which the road is built. To prevent erosion, ditches are dug, and culverts (large drainage pipes under the road) are installed to carry water away from the roadbed.

In rural areas, the roadbed is often covered with gravel. Busy roads and highways are hard-surfaced with asphalt or concrete. Asphalt — a mixture of coal tar, sand, and gravel — is heated and laid on the roadbed. Concrete is a mixture of sand, gravel, and crushed stone held together by water and cement. Asphalt and

Michele discusses a blueprint with an on-site supervisor. "Each job starts with a blueprint, which is like a recipe," says Michele. "A blueprint even includes a shopping list of everything needed to build a road."

In the background of this photograph are two highways that used to meet at a stop sign. Because there were many accidents at this intersection, an overpass is being built. Michele is responsible for making sure that the overpass is constructed according to the blueprint, or plan.

concrete provide smooth and long-lasting road surfaces.

"Asphalt was first used to waterproof ships," comments Michele. "In the mid-1800s, the French government experimented by using asphalt to pave roads. The idea caught on and is now used around the world!"

Getting started

1. At home, do hands-on projects such as building model ships and airplanes. If possible, help design and build a deck or an interlocking brick walkway.
2. Do engineering-related Science Fair projects, for example, experiments with weight-bearing. Test different ways of folding a piece of paper so that it holds increasingly more weight.
3. Learn about famous historic roads and how roads can influence economic development. A librarian can help you gather information on this topic.
4. Take industrial arts and computer classes. Computer programs can simplify many of the mathematical calculations necessary for road construction.
5. In high school, plan to take mathematics, physics, and chemistry, and don't forget English and geography. Engineers need good writing skills. Studying geography will give you an understanding of how climate affects roads.

Bob Izumi — Fishing Pro

"I go fishing at least 180 days every year — and people pay me to do it!" Bob Izumi smiles. "When I fish in tournaments, I can win thousands of dollars. A camera crew takes pictures of me fishing, and I get paid for this as well. If someone had told me in high school that I would find a job like this, I would never have believed it!"

In fishing tournaments, anglers compete to catch fish in a specified time. Because Bob does well in tournaments, companies pay him to endorse their outdoor products, such as boats, motors, and fishing tackle. Now that Bob has become well-known, tournaments take up about 30 percent of his time.

"Besides fishing in tournaments," says Bob, "I also give seminars at outdoor shows and special events sponsored by outdoor companies. For example, I might talk about a useful fishing lure and show slides of the different ways to use it. I then show video clips of the lure in action."

"Don't expect to get something for nothing," Bob warns. "In return for the use of fancy boats and equipment, I'm expected to advertise these products for the manufacturers."

Fishing tips

About half of Bob's work involves hosting radio and TV shows. "My radio 'shorts' are one-minute tips on a specific subject, such as how weather affects fish," Bob explains, "These are scripted ahead of time and I record them in a rented studio. I produce 130 shorts each year. Recording them takes five full days of studio time. It's a lot of work, but it's good exposure, because 70 radio stations use the tips.

"The most time-consuming part of my job is producing 26 TV programs a year. I sell these shows to more than

28 stations. Each half-hour show is put together from four to five hours of videotape."

Learning from others

Bob credits much of his fishing success to his people skills! Anglers often ask him questions about fishing. During these conversations, Bob learns useful information, such as the location of a good fishing hole. "It's important to listen to people," Bob says, "and to ask them questions while you're answering theirs. Intelligent people ask questions — and benefit from the answers!"

Bob laughs about the light-colored "mask" around his eyes. "Normally, I wear polarized sunglasses to reduce the glare bouncing off the water. Sunglasses also help me see fish underwater. I wear them so much, I now have a 'reverse raccoon mask'"!

Getting started

1. Read fishing magazines. Learn everything you can about the appearance, habitats, and habits of fish.
2. Join outdoor clubs. Get involved in conservation projects, such as stocking lakes with fish.
3. Go fishing with experienced anglers. If you can't fish with them, watch them from a distance. What do they do that helps them catch more fish?
4. Take a boating course. Learn the regulations for navigating small boats in inland waters. Learn how to read charts and maps.
5. Join a public speaking club and learn to speak in front of a group.
6. In high school, take courses in biology, geography, business, and communications.

Classified Advertising

HELP WANTED

COMPUTER OPERATIONS SUPERVISOR

Retail chain with P.O.S. (DOS), back office system (UNIX), accounting experience. Debra 444-4444

SENIOR Computer Artist needed as a Software Operator. Must have a minimum of 18 months' experience with similar software. 35 hr. work week, rotating shift work involved. Salary $36,400/yr. Please forward resumé to Box 2040, The Daily News, City, Province/State.

UNIX/C Programmer. Some international travel. Please call 647-2105.

LABORATORY Technician for a time research position at local hospital. B.Sc. or M.Sc. and experience in molecular biology required. Call 357-1492.

PHYSIOTHERAPIST

The Community Health Center is seeking a part-time therapist. This health center offers a multidisciplinary approach with special focus on Seniors, Education, and Health Promotion. Competitive salary with excellent benefits. Candidates must be eligible for registration with the Society of Physiotherapists.

Please send resumé by October 16, 19— Community Health Center 30 Smith St., Unit 201, City, Province/State; Attention: Executive Coordinator

Position Available

An inner-city Community Health Center, with community and clinical activities, is looking for experienced staff for the following positions:

Nurse Practitioner: B.Sc.N. or equivalent. Experience in community-based primary health care and program planning. Strong clinical skills required.

Health Promoter: Health promotion degree or equivalent. Demonstrated success in developing and implementing health promotion programs at a community level. Good communication and group facilitation skills required.

Community Health Worker: Social services degree or equivalent. Demonstrated success in developing and implementing community-based projects. Grassroots advocacy and community organizing experience an asset. Familiarity with community health issues and resources a must.

Successful candidates will have:

- experience with any of the following: street people, ex-psychiatric patients, low-income people, families in crisis, and/or immigrants.
- the ability to work well both independently, and as part of a multidisciplinary team.
- multicultural experience and/or knowledge of other languages

Send your reply, indicating the position you wish to apply for, to: Carol Klim, Program Coordinator, Central Community Health Center; 3 Augusta Avenue, City, Province/State; Fax 363-2115.

KEYBOARD DEPT. MANAGER

Responsible for inventory management sales and marketing. Must be hardworking, with sales experience and product knowledge in some of the following: Home Keyboard, Pro Synthesis Home Recording, and Music Software. Sales Position also available. Forward resumé to: **MusicComp, 392 East St., City, Province/State**

Electronics Engineer

Traffic Systems Company Limited requires an Electronics Engineer. The successful candidate...

Ma... Sys... ited Prov... 998-2...

Apprentice Leader

APPRENTICE LEADER

Almaguin Trail Rides requires an **Apprentice Leader** for July and August. Working under the supervision of the stable owner, the apprentice will feed 25 horses, clean the stable and the tack, lead trail rides, and assist with riding instruction for beginners. Horseback-riding experience essential.

Apply in writing to

**Audrey Gottlieb
Almaguin Trail Rides
Canter Road, R.R. #1
Horse Haven
Province/State, Postal/Zip Code**

Manager, Environmental Services

Fuels, Inc. is seeking a bright, self-directed professional with a broad understanding of environmental issues to assist in the development and coordination of company environmental policies and programs.

... include participation in environmental assessments ... of new facility construction, review of operating procedures, waste management strategies, advising company departments and regions with respect to compliance with environmental legislation, environmental auditing, and monitoring ... research and government ... ..., Inc.

The ... minimum of 7 years ... familiarity with ... distributor. Strong ... ive salary and ... consideration, ...

... of Mechanical Engineering Tech-op Ltd. 402 Maple St., City, Province/State (Tel ... 7182; Fax ...

... all applicants for applying. However, only those under consideration will be contacted.

... the distribution of ... security/fire/s... sy... We are currently se...ng ...vidual to sell su... This ...tion will be bas... ur ce... office and will ... approx...ely 20% field... Qualifica...s include a ... sales bac...round in the ...ctronic security/fire industry and strong interpersonal skills. For consideration and a local interview, applicants should forward resumés, complete with salary history, to: **Mr. R. Treed Security Inc. 319 Southfield Drive City, Province/State**

Pharmacist

You will be responsible for delivery of all inpatient, outpatient, and retail pharmacy services. This position requires a professional designation, and a minimum of 2 years' related experience within a retail or hospital pharmacy operation. Excellent communication skills and the ability to work independently are essential to your success in this job. The location will appeal to individuals who enjoy extensive outdoor recreation activities, including kayaking, boating, exploring many small islands, and fishing. Along with this wonderful, close-to-nature environment, the successful candidate will enjoy a competitive compensation package and a subsidized housing package. Qualified candidates are invited to apply to:

Administrator, R.W. Large Memorial Hospital City, Province/State, Postal Code/Zip Code; Tel: (000) 357-2314, Fax: (000) 357-2315

Who got the job?

Finding a job

The first step to success in any career is getting a job. But how do you go about finding one?

- Talk with family, friends, and neighbors, and let them know what jobs interest you.

- Respond to "Help Wanted" ads in newspapers.

- Post an advertisement of your skills on a community bulletin board.

- Register at government employment offices or private employment agencies.
- Contact potential employers by phone or in person.

- Send out inquiry letters to companies and follow up with phone calls.

A job application usually consists of a letter and a resumé (a summary of your work experience, including volunteer work, as well as your qualifications for thc job). Some job advertisements ask you to apply in person and to bring your resumé with you; others ask you to send in your letter and resumé by mail.

Activity

A job on horseback

Read the job ad on the opposite page. Almaguin Trail Rides needs an apprentice leader to help out during the summer. How would you apply for the job?

The trail riding company received many applications for this job. Almaguin's owner-manager, Audrey Gottlieb, had time to interview only a few applicants, so she chose the ones whose resumés showed the best qualifications for the position. She granted interviews to Joe Cardinal and Tammy Cheung. Their letters of application and their resumés, as well as the notes that Audrey Gottlieb made during their interviews, are shown on pages 46 and 47.

Procedure

Read the letters, the resumés, and Audrey Gottlieb's notes on the two applicants, Joe and Tammy. List what you see as each applicant's strengths and weaknesses. Do both applicants qualify for the job? Which person would you hire? Why? You may feel that more experience is necessary for the job, and, therefore, hire neither of these applicants.

Challenge

How would you perform in a job interview? Role-play the interview for the job as apprentice leader, with a friend acting the part of Audrey Gottlieb. Then reverse roles. Audrey Gottlieb was especially impressed with Joe's questions about how she runs her business. Role-play how to ask an employer perceptive questions during an interview. Role-playing will give you practice asking and answering questions appropriately, so that when you apply for a job, you'll have a good chance of getting it!

Tammy Cheung's application and interview

Resumé

Tammy Cheung
2789 Ralston Parkway, Apartment 1007
Cliffton, Province/State; Postal/Zip Code
Telephone: (716) 555-2208

Job Experience

Groom, 19— - present
(Part-time) Cliffton Downs Racetrack
Supervised by the head groom, I walk horses after e___
race. On non-race nights, I brush 10 horses and much ___
their stalls.

Library Assistant, 19— - present
Cliffton Secondary School Library
I check out and reshelve books.

Housework, 19— - 19—
Provided regular babysitting and housework assistance to
three neighboring families. Supervised children aged six
months to 10 years.

Education
Final year, Cliffton Secondary School; my strong subjects are
chemistry, biology, phys. ed., and English.

Special Skills, Interests, and Awards
- Bilingual (English and Chinese)
- Outdoor Leadership Course, Deer Lake Girl Scout Camp
- Horseback riding, woodworking, hiking
- Third Place, National Essay Contest,
Science Educators of America.

References: On request

2789 Ralston Parkway
Apartment 1007
Cliffton, Province/State
Postal/Zip Code

June 4, 19—

Audrey Gottlieb
Almaguin Trail Rides
Canter Road, R.R. #1
Horse Haven, Province/State
Postal/Zip Code

Dear Ms. Gottlieb,
I would like to apply for the position of Apprentice
Leader, which was advertised in the Summerclouds Beacon
Star on Friday, May 28, 19—.
As you will note from the enclosed resumé, I have had
some work experience at the local racetrack, where I walk
horses after each race. In addition, I learned how to ride
horses at teen camp. Last summer, I started learning how
to jump.
Although I do not live in the Horse Haven area, my aunt
has agreed that if I get the job, I can stay with her for the
summer.
I would love a summer job working with horses, and
would like to meet with you to discuss this interesting
position. Please contact me by telephone after 6:00 p.m.
at (716) 555-2208.

Sincerely,

Tammy Cheung

Tammy Cheung

Interview: Tammy Cheung

- One hour late, but phoned to say she was delayed by an accident.
- Wore a blouse and skirt, had riding pants and boots with her.

WHY DOES SHE WANT THE JOB?

- likes horses, saved own money to pay for riding lessons, wants to learn to ride well.

WHAT DOES SHE THINK OF HER WORK AT THE RACE TRACK?

- "great": learned a lot about horses.

CONFIRMED

Joe Cardinal's application and interview

Joe Cardinal
R.R. #3
Summerclouds, Province/State
Postal/Zip Code

0, 19—

y Gottlieb
uin Trail Rides
r Road, R.R. #1
e Haven, Province/State
al/Zip Code

r Ms. Gottlieb,

sh to apply for the position of Apprentice Leader as
ertised in the Summerclouds Beacon Star on Friday,
/ 28, 19—. Please find enclosed my resume for your review
d consideration.

For the past two years, I have been a junior counselor at a
ing camp called Treetop Acres. Before that, I attended
imp Kohoe for three summers. At this camp, I learned how
o clean tack and muck out a stall. I had a riding lesson every
morning. In the afternoon, I rode on the trails with my group.

In elementary school, I volunteered to groom horses at the
Wasauksing Association for Riding for the Disabled (W.A.R.D.).
I am still a W.A.R.D. volunteer.

I love working with horses, and would appreciate meeting
you for an interview. I can be reached any time after dark at
555-9440. I work at W.A.R.D. after school, helping to teach
riding to people who have disabilities.

Sincerely yours,

Joe Cardinal

Joe Cardinal

Resumé

Joe Cardinal
R.R. #3
Summerclouds, Province/State
Postal/Zip Code
Telephone: (203) 555-9440

Education
Final year, Summerclouds High School;
taking courses in general science, physical education,
geography, mathematics, English, art, and history

Work Experience
March 19— - present
• Volunteer, Wasauksing Association for Riding for the Disabled
c/o Box 725, Summerclouds, Province/State, Postal/Zip Code
groom and exercise horses, and lead horses during
class instruction.

Summers, 19— - 19—
• Junior counselor; assisted with the riding program;
stable and tack cleaning; fed, groomed, saddled, and
exercised horses
Treetop Acres, R.R. #1, McKellar, Province/State
Postal/Zip Code

Special Skills and Interests
• Fluent French and Ojibway (spoken)
• Bicycle repairs
• Wilderness camping
• Volunteer, Lake Trout Rehabilitation Program

References available upon request

Interview: Joe Cardinal
• On time, wore sports shirt,
casual pants, and riding boots.
Asked to see stables.

WHY DOES HE WANT THE JOB?
• loves working outdoors, especially
with beginning riders; does
volunteer work with W.A.R.D.

DID HE ENJOY HIS WORK AT TREETOP ACRES?
• yes—liked working with horses
everyday; learned a lot from
head instructor.

Index

Credits

(l = left; r = right; t = top; b = bottom; c = center; bl = bottom left; br = bottom right)

All photographs by Helen Mason, except 5(l), 8 Ontario Hydro Forestry Trade Reference Manual; 5(r) Scott Madahbee; 11, 12(t), 13, 14 Ellen Heale, INCO Ltd.; 18(b) Trudy Rising; 19(b) David Rising; 23, 24(t,b) Nigel Shaw; 25(r,l) Bowles & Söber; 28, 30(t) Glenn Hare; 31 James D. Rising; 34 Becky Kudloo; 35, 36, 37, 38 Atmospheric Environment Service, Government of Canada.